LINCOLN CHRISTIAN COLLEGE AND SEMINARY

P9-DIB-074

Social workers . . . are raised by experience and training to distrust money, business and capitalism. We develop a mind-set that views money as evil. Grow up.

— Jed Emerson (from *The New Social Entrepreneurs*)

Too many nonprofit organizations are financially stagnant, raising and distributing funds the same way they have for decades . . . . A nonprofit that is run for profit sounds like a contradiction in terms. But it doesn't have to be.

— Bill Shore (from *Revolution of the Heart*)

The Challenge

The nonprofit sector today is peopled by millions of talented, compassionate men and women dedicated to helping others. One of every seven American workers is employed by a nonprofit.

During the past 30 years, as social problems worsened, these men and women have met one challenge after another. They are the living embodiment of a precious American value — helping your neighbor when he or she can no longer make it alone.

But the nonprofit sector is in trouble. And the pressures today are daunting. For example:

Reductions continue in public sector support. Government spending on social services and the arts is plummeting, at every level — state and federal funding collapsed by a total of 23 percent during the 1980s — and we are in the midst of another wave of reductions today.

Fluctuations persist in individual and corporate giving. Individual giving sank by nearly 20 percent during the first two years of the 1990s and has not yet rallied completely. Wealthy Americans are now giving only four percent of their annual income to charity compared with seven percent during the

Contents

© National Center for Nonprofit Boards
This publication may not be reproduced without permission.

99024

1

1980s. Corporate philanthropy has increasingly been replaced by cause-related marketing and has diminished substantially since its high-water mark in the early 1980s.

More nonprofits are competing for available funds. At the same time, the number of nonprofits has exploded: For every three that existed just seven years ago, there are four today, and they are all gathering at the same watering hole. As one foundation executive recently said, "there're just too damn many nonprofits out there, and they're tripping over each other." There is increased pressure from funders and others to merge or downsize, along with increased demands for accountability and marketplace realities such as managed care. These factors are further complicated by other forms of institutional stress such as rising costs, depleted reserves and staff burnout.

Many more people are in need. As recently as 15 years ago, few nonprofits were dealing with such problems as AIDS, homelessness, or crack babies. Today, among many of the sector's other burdens, Catholic Charities is serving four times as many people as it did a decade ago, millions of people are losing their welfare benefits, the population of frail elderly people continues to mushroom, and funding for the National Endowment for the Arts is constantly in jeopardy.

And the reputation of the sector has been buffeted repeatedly. From the United Way of America's William Aramony scandal of 1990 to the Foundation for New Era Philanthropy Ponzi scheme of 1995, nonprofits have suffered by association. There has been a loss of confidence in the management of nonprofits, and recent Gallup polls reveal that *one in three Americans believes the nonprofit sector should be eliminated* because nonprofits are perceived as unethical, inefficient, and ineffective.

This is not the nonprofit world of the 1950s or even the 1980s. But it *is* the world in which we are living, and it poses a daunting challenge for nonprofit boards of directors.

The Pioneers

Volunteers and staff members have taken yeoman's strides to meet the challenge, but they are continuing to fall further and further behind. The very survival of many social service, arts, and other nonprofit organizations is at stake.

But nonprofits *must* survive and continue to serve, and in recent years organizations across the country have begun responding to the challenge in a new way. What we are beginning to see is a tectonic shift in the culture of the nonprofit sector, in the way it behaves, in the way it thinks about itself, and in the way it is funded. The shift is shattering old definitions, uprooting careers, and changing the very nature of the job.

This new movement is being led by a new type of social servant, a growing body of pioneers who are telling us to shed the old definitions and to take responsibility for our own survival — to stop depending so heavily on contributions and government support and to explore new ways to fund the organization's mission.

These men and women are social entrepreneurs, and they are changing the face of the nonprofit sector.

© National Center for Nonprofit Boards

Simply put, "social entrepreneurs" are nonprofit executives and board members who pay increasing attention to market forces *without* losing sight of their underlying missions, and that balancing act is the heart and soul of the movement. These people are being asked to somehow balance moral imperatives and the profit motive, and many are making it work. By adopting entrepreneurial strategies, they have been able to:

◆ sort through everything they do from both a mission *and* an earned-income perspective;

◆ expand their most effective and needed programs and productively dispose of the others;

◆ start business ventures rooted in the core competencies of their organizations; and

◆ become increasingly self-sufficient financially and therefore less dependent on government and charity.

For example:

◆ John DuRand began working in the mid-1960s with seven people who were mentally retarded. By the time he retired during the winter of 1997, Minnesota Diversified Industries had become a $57 million not-for-profit business employing more than 1,000 people.

◆ Margaret Cossette started in the mid-1970s with six part-time employees and a $16,000 grant. Today, Missouri Home Care is a $10 million for-profit business providing nonmedical care to more than 2,500 elderly people in 39 rural counties.

◆ Dr. Mimi Silbert helped start the Delancey Street Foundation with $1,000 from a loan shark in the early 1970s. Today the foundation operates nine profitable small businesses, employs only former convicts and drug addicts, and has returned more than 10,000 people to the mainstream.

◆ Bill Kling's entrepreneurial adventure at Minnesota Public Radio started when Garrison Keillor off-handedly promised to send his listeners a calendar if they responded to an informal survey (at the time, no such calendar existed). Today the station operates a for-profit subsidiary that generates more than $200 million in annual gross revenue.

◆ Rick Surpin and his colleagues started brainstorming ways to create jobs for African-American and Latino women in 1984. Today Cooperative Home Care Associates is a $5 million business employing more than 300 women in the South Bronx alone, captured the National Business Enterprise Trust award in 1992, has been the subject of a case study at Harvard, has launched a for-profit subsidiary, and has expanded into four other cities.

But it's not necessary to start a business venture in order to be successful as a social entrepreneur. Most entrepreneurial efforts start small — and they are driven by a double bottom line, a mixture of both "mission" and "money."

The "Mission" Goals

Social entrepreneurs have two "mission" goals: To sharpen their organizational focus and to expand their impact. When Jack Welch took over as CEO at General Electric in 1981, he asked management guru Peter Drucker to tell him the single most important thing he could do to improve the company. The answer was simple: *If you are not the best or the second best supplier of a product or service, you should stop providing it!* In other words, *stop trying to be all things to all people.*

His advice runs against the grain of the traditional nonprofit mentality. We see people in pain, we start a program. We see somebody else in pain, we start another program. Most nonprofit executives will admit that they are trying to do too many things for too many people. They're searching for a way to sharpen their focus by identifying their most effective and needed programs and by productively disposing of their more peripheral programs, either by finding a home for them in other agencies, by allowing them to gradually phase out, or by eliminating those that are wreaking financial havoc on the rest of the organization. Drucker calls it "organized abandonment," and it is the first and most important step toward sharpening an organization's focus. For example, Child Center of Our Lady, a St. Louis nonprofit serving children with behavioral challenges, eliminated seven of its 15 programs and entirely changed its mission.

One important caveat: *Being a social entrepreneur does not mean eliminating a program just because it loses money.* If a nonprofit is the best or the only provider of a program that is critically needed, it has an obligation to continue the program, and a managerial challenge to find other sources of revenue to cover the cost.

However, it makes no sense for five or six nonprofits in the same geographic area to deliver the same product or service. If one of your programs ranks third or lower, let it go! Hand it over to number one or number two and concentrate on the areas where *you* are the leader.

Despite having fewer programs, social entrepreneurs are still able to **expand** *their impact — the second mission goal.* Because they are able to concentrate more of their resources on fewer programs, they have more time to develop positioning strategies and marketing plans that work and are able to selectively add new programs to meet the emerging needs of their communities. For example, Children's Home Society of Minnesota eliminated three of its seven divisions — but within a single year had opened four new facilities, acquired part of another agency, and raised its operating budget by 17 percent.

The "Money" Goals

Despite the importance of mission goals, however, most people who think about entrepreneurship in the nonprofit sector think first about financial returns. This is understandable. According to INDEPENDENT SECTOR, the average nonprofit in 1977 had more than three months of operating capital in reserve at any given time; by 1989 the average reserve had diminished to less than four days. Recent INDEPENDENT SECTOR studies have

© National Center for Nonprofit Boards

also revealed that the average nonprofit nationwide still produces less than 15 percent of its revenue from earned income.

Nonprofits can generate earned income either from their current programs or from entirely new activities, some of which can then be structured as programs and others as business ventures. In either case, *the primary goal is to become increasingly self-sufficient financially* and therefore less dependent on government subsidies and charity. But the concept of "earned income" is a confusing one to many people in the nonprofit sector, and it is important to emphasize a few key points before describing the levels of self-sufficiency that might be possible.

To begin with, *"earned income" implies a quid pro quo arrangement in which there is a direct exchange of service or product for monetary value.* This definition includes such things as:

◆ **Fee-for-service payments,** either directly from clients or indirectly from a third party such as Medicaid or an insurance program. Such services may include counseling, residential housing, or outpatient medical clinics.

◆ **Revenue from product sales, consulting contracts, tuition, rent, or lease payments.** Museums increase their revenues through gift shop sales, while universities create extra income by expanding contract research.

◆ **Traditional forms of revenue generation from activities such as book publishing and conferences.** For many nonprofits, publishing and conferences serve a public education function and occasionally pay for themselves.

But the following types of revenue do *not* qualify as earned income: Undesignated, unrestricted, or general operating grants; contributions from individuals; bequests; sponsorship of special events; most types of cause-related marketing; and so on.

That said, there are three types of increasingly ambitious financial goals that nonprofits can pursue if they adopt entrepreneurial strategies:

Incremental gains
(for individual programs or entire organizations)

This goal can be achieved by *any* nonprofit, and it can start to happen almost immediately: A reasonable three- to five-year objective would be to increase earned income by an amount equal to 15 percent of the organization's annual operating budget. For example:

◆ **The Metropolitan Atlanta Council on Alcohol and Drugs (MACAD)** has gone from $30,000 to $300,000 per year in earned income, in part by capitalizing on the Internet. The organization provides information and referral services over the phone for people seeking a substance abuse treatment facility. Initially available only in a binder, the information was later computerized for internal purposes and now is updated every week on the Internet, with MACAD selling access to its database to the courts for $100,000 per year.

◆ **The Minnesota Orchestral Association** will soon be covering about 10 percent of its annual operating costs from the profits generated by a single new business venture. The orchestra considered more than 100 potential ideas before settling on one that would help it create a new generation of classical music lovers, an important part of its mission. The new business is based on the concept of a videotaped "story concert" that combines well-known children's books with animation and original orchestral music. The videos are aimed at eight- to ten-year-old children, and the first production received the American Library Association's Andrew Carnegie Medal for Excellence in Children's Video, which is given to only one children's video in the country each year.

Self-sufficiency
(for specific programs or business ventures, and, on rare occasions, for entire organizations)

This goal can be achieved by *some* nonprofits, but it will usually take a considerable period of time. For example:

◆ **The Kansas City chapter of the American Red Cross** discovered during the mid-1980s that fewer and fewer people were coming to its walk-in service centers because they were located in older parts of town (only about 200 people a month were visiting each center). In order to reverse that trend, the chapter decided to reposition itself by opening a retail store that would sell safety equipment in a perimeter shopping mall and by locating a service center immediately next door. The intent was to break even with the store and to generate foot traffic for the center. Within five years the chapter had three successful stores and the average foot traffic at each of the adjoining centers was 2,700 people per month.

◆ Among many other programs, the **Bidwell Vocational Training School** in Pittsburgh trains welfare recipients, unemployed steelworkers, and inner-city teenagers to become chefs. The reputation of the program grew during the early 1990s when students started providing catering services to individuals and organizations on an informal basis. Eventually, Bidwell realized it had a business opportunity and started a separate venture that today generates more than $3 million in annual gross revenue and handles culinary contracts at the airport, the science center, and other locations around the city.

◆ When Charlie Graham arrived at **St. Vincent de Paul Rehabilitation Center** in Portland, Oregon, in 1985, it was a $1 million sheltered workshop that was 80 percent subsidized. When he left in 1995 it was a $10 million affirmative business that was 90 percent self-sufficient. Graham triggered the transformation by immediately changing the mission of the organization and then doing something nonprofits rarely do: He bought an existing, for-profit company and hired the previous owners to train his employees.

Significant profitability and growth
(for spin-off business ventures or entire organizations)

This goal can be achieved only by a *very few* nonprofits, and it will usually take them a very long time. For example:

© National Center for Nonprofit Boards

◆ **Housing Works** is a New York City nonprofit providing housing, advocacy and support services for homeless people living with AIDS and HIV. Seven years ago, as the AIDS industry began to emerge, Housing Works committed itself to providing jobs for its clients. Today the organization operates three upscale thrift shops, a used book café, and a dollar store. Annual revenues are about $5 million, with a profit margin of 30 percent (the $1.5 million in profit covers about 12 percent of the parent organization's annual budget).

◆ When Gary Mulhair became President of **Pioneer Human Services** in 1984, the Seattle nonprofit had a heavily subsidized budget of approximately $4 million. Today it's a profitable, $38 million organization providing transitional and long-term housing, job training, and employment for people who have been in prison or in alcohol and drug treatment programs. Most of the 3,000 to 4,500 clients served each year work for one of Pioneer's many businesses, which include a light-metal fabrication facility, a wholesale food business serving nearly 400 food banks in 20 states, a corporate cafeteria for the Starbucks company, an institutional food business preparing about 1,000 meals a day, a property management company, a hotel in downtown Seattle, and a number of others.

◆ The mission of New Jersey's largest community development and nonprofit housing corporation is to provide services for Newark residents and to create employment by placing city residents into jobs that deliver those services. **New Community Corporation** has been around for 25 years and today runs a nursing home that employs 240 people, a day care center that employs another 240, and a home health care program that provides jobs for 160. The organization also operates a number of retail stores and has become involved in banking, real estate management, institutional food services, comprehensive job training, shopping center management, and a fine-dining restaurant. All told, New Community employs about 1,500 people, has its own credit union and business loan fund, and is generating more than $25 million in revenue each year.

◆ **Vitas Health Care Corporation** began providing hospice care to a single individual in the basement of a Miami church in the mid-1970s. Today it's a $250-million-a-year business that has already served more than 75,000 people in nine states.

Potential Pitfalls

The nonprofits most prepared for entrepreneurship today are those that have been the most innovative during the past 10 or 15 years. Their challenge is to make the transition from a culture of innovation to a culture of entrepreneurship; however, the journey can be fraught with danger. In order to make sure the organization's expectations are realistic and its commitment sufficient, the nonprofit's board should spend some time at the beginning of the process attempting to identify potential pitfalls, which tend to fall into at least four categories:

Concerns about the basic concept

◆ Does this activity make us look as if we're trying to earn money off the backs of the poor?

◆ What happens to quality when we start emphasizing the bottom line?

◆ Are we setting up a two-tiered system that ignores the people who can't afford to pay?

Each of these questions, and dozens of others like them, is legitimate and needs to be addressed by every board member before the organization proceeds with any earned income plan.

Concerns about getting started

◆ We are already running at more than full speed. How can we possibly find time and personnel to take on this project?

◆ Do we have the right people on staff to make this work?

◆ Do we have any spare cash?

The "resource" question becomes an insurmountable stumbling block for many nonprofits, yet history shows that when a nonprofit really wants to do something, it manages to find the people, the time, the money, and the energy it needs.

Concerns about failure

◆ Will it cause a financial disaster?

◆ Will it severely damage our reputation?

◆ Will it deplete our energy and resources?

The possibility of failure is very real. Personal careers can crash and burn. There are no guarantees.

Concerns about success

◆ Will we lose our hearts when we find our wallets? "All the people who came to do *good* and stayed to do *well!*"

◆ How can we protect our nonprofit status?

◆ Can we manage such rapid growth?

What happens once you succeed? Simple. Somebody raises the bar.

Critical Success Factors

In spite of these valid concerns, more and more boards are taking their organizations in the direction of social entrepreneurship, either by adopting internal earned income strategies (designed primarily to cover more of an organization's costs, not necessarily to turn a profit) or by creating social purpose business ventures (whose primary purpose *is* to make a profit).

 © National Center for Nonprofit Boards

Here are 12 critical success factors that have been identified by the pioneers in the field:

1. Candor

The first raw material for social entrepreneurs is candor, and it is probably the toughest challenge for any entrepreneur. Starting a new venture, or even an earned income strategy, is difficult enough without being honest about your product or service, your market, your competition, your resources, and numerous other factors that help determine success or failure. The mantra here is very simple: "Beware of yourself!"

2. Passion

Please, do not attempt to become a social entrepreneur because it is something you think you "should" do, or because your funders push you in that direction.

Unless both board and staff are ignited by the prospect, unless it is something that almost everyone can believe in, entrepreneurship is probably not for you, at least not at the present time. But if your board and staff members can carefully acknowledge every potential pitfall — and most of them can still feel a strong desire to proceed — then it may be worthwhile to give it a try, even if it requires a considerable leap of faith.

Only you know whether your organization possesses sufficient quantities of candor and passion; both are invisible to the outside world at the beginning of the process — but their absence will quickly become apparent to others thereafter.

3. Clarity

The third raw material is clarity, and it has two components. First, why is your organization heading down this path at all? What are the driving forces behind this shift in direction? It is important that board members come to a consensus on this issue before starting the planning process, because your organization will be intensely scrutinized and the board will need to have consistent, compelling answers ready for its critics (and there *will* be critics!). Here are four rationales that a number of nonprofits have found to be both useful and energizing:

◆ **"Mission"** — We're doing this because it will enable us to serve more people;

◆ **"Survival"** — We're doing this because our more traditional sources of funding are drying up;

◆ **"Opportunity"** — We're doing this because the market is beckoning — we're already experiencing a demand for our service; and

◆ **"Freedom"** — If we can generate more of our own money, we won't be so tied to the priorities and restrictions imposed on us by others.

Those four words — mission, survival, opportunity, and freedom — can become the rallying cry for the entire effort and a major reason for your organization's success.

But there is another aspect of clarity that is equally important, even though it may force you onto uncertain ground, and that is the answer to the following question: "What will success look like?" It is important to define some long-term goals before you begin; if you don't, you will never be able to demonstrate your success to anybody (including yourselves) and you will be vulnerable to false prophets along the way.

4. Commitment

The fourth raw material is commitment, because the typical nonprofit is besieged by crises. Unless the board *and* the staff declare that entrepreneurial planning is a priority, it will be swept aside by the flood of day-to-day demands. Unfortunately, too many boards are reluctant to commit because they are either risk-averse or searching for a quick fix. Both attitudes are understandable, but they conflict with marketplace realities.

The fact is, some earned income strategies will fail. Unless the board is willing to accept that fact and take some chances, it should not proceed at all! And the board must also be willing to take a longer view: Many board members think in terms of "cost" rather than "investment," and are reluctant to proceed unless they can see a rapid return. Entrepreneurship doesn't work that way. It takes time.

5. Courage

Becoming a social entrepreneur takes courage, both personal and institutional. Above all, it takes the courage to change, because every nonprofit has an organizational "culture" that gets in the way. That culture exists for both board and staff whether they are aware of it or not. It is a collection of shared values that defines who we are, what we stand for, how we should treat our clients, and so on. These values are rarely spoken aloud but are self-evident to new employees, who pick them up by osmosis within a few days or weeks.

Culture eats change for breakfast. Perhaps the single greatest obstacle for nonprofits attempting to adopt entrepreneurial strategies is the traditional nonprofit mentality, a mindset that not only says we should be all things to all people, but simultaneously insists that "we're not supposed to make money!" This deeply ingrained mentality views philanthropy as the bedrock of the organization. But social entrepreneurs reject that concept out of hand: To them, earned income is the primary financing strategy, not philanthropy.

The obstacle here is paradigm paralysis, a phrase coined by corporate trainer Joel Barker. As Barker points out, paradigms can be useful tools. They give us a way to make sense of the world, to establish a set of rules and regulations, and to organize and interpret incoming data. But a paradigm can be a double-edged sword. Blinders are slapped into place and we begin to interpret the new information according to our preconceptions. We become frozen and change becomes our enemy.

Institutional paralysis can be overcome with a sufficient dose of courage. But occasionally it takes something dramatic. A few years ago, when the board of directors of a nonprofit in Louisville, Kentucky, offered its leading candidate the job as CEO, he realized the existing makeup of the board worked against entrepreneurship and agreed to accept the position only if every member of the board resigned. They agreed.

Still another CEO, who ran a sheltered workshop in Minnesota, decided to change the basic values of his organization. He invited his 11 senior managers to a St. Paul hotel where he wined and dined them, asked them to sit down — and then fired them all. Five minutes later he passed out application forms. "Starting tomorrow," he said, "we are no longer a rehab agency, we're a business. Starting tomorrow, we no longer have clients, we have employees. And starting tomorrow, you are no longer clinicians, you are business manag-

© National Center for Nonprofit Boards

ers. If you can get your minds and hearts and souls around that concept, I want you back. If you can't, I'll help you find a job somewhere else."

Nine of the 11 returned to their jobs. Two could not accept the philosophical shift. But, from that day, the culture of the organization changed and the primary goal became the operation of a viable business.

In sum, changing the culture of an organization is no easy task. As board members, you need to ask yourselves: Are you capable of making tough decisions? Are you willing to take some risks? And are you ready to take the heat? If you suspect that either you or the organization will waffle, wait until you are completely ready and work on the areas of softness before you proceed.

6. Core values

The sixth raw material addresses the key question voiced by board members and nonprofit executives: "Just how *is* it possible to balance mission and money?" The only lasting answer is to identify a set of four or five core values that are clearly articulated, institutionalized, and constantly reinforced.

Starting down the path of entrepreneurship means you will be tempted by things you have never been tempted by before, and you will need an internal sense of balance to help you resist them. Some social entrepreneurs are not able to resist temptation. Just watch *60 Minutes* for a month and you will see investigative reporters rip into social entrepreneurs with the same zeal they normally reserve for corporate raiders.

The board should identify core values before beginning. Make sure those values can be quantified. Build them into your strategic and your annual operating plans. Monitor them religiously. Measure your progress at least once a year and trumpet the results.

7. Customer focus

One of the most difficult shifts in perspective required of any nonprofit adopting entrepreneurial strategies is to understand its audience.

When I worked as an executive for a Fortune 100 company, it took me at least five years to fully internalize the difference between "market push" and "market pull." If you start with your products and services, then go out in search of a buyer, you're trying to *push* your way into the market. But if you start with the people you are serving, find out what they need, then build those products and services, they will be *pulling* you into the market. Good ideas pull you *toward* them.

Unfortunately, most nonprofit executives also have a tough time trying to internalize the difference between market push and market pull. No matter how many times nonprofit executives claim to understand, they frequently begin by talking about "*our* programs, *our* plan, *our* staff, *our* needs, *our* board." Too many are guilty of starting with organizational needs rather than the needs of the marketplace.

8. A willingness to plan

John Wooden, who led his UCLA basketball team to 10 national championships, once said that "failing to prepare is preparing to fail." According to the Small Business

Administration, 90 percent of business failures are caused by management mistakes, not by competitors, changes in the market, or other external factors.

The planning process for an earned income effort is straightforward and based on common sense. Unfortunately, many people in the nonprofit sector are impatient and are tempted to skip steps. Don't. The stakes are too high.

One of the most important aspects of planning, of course, is getting off on the right foot. Here are three suggestions to help you do so:

◆ **Ask for help.**
   Appoint a planning team made up of board, staff, and outsiders who are willing to dedicate themselves to this project. Be sure the planning team includes some "business mentors," proven entrepreneurs who have successfully built their own small or medium-sized businesses. They'll provide a reality check that is invaluable. Bring in some "wild cards" as well, people who may not know much about your agency or even about business *per se*. Tell them their job is to ask all the "dumb" questions out loud, to probe the areas others might neglect because they are too close to the table. You might be surprised at what you learn.

◆ **Put somebody in charge.**
   The team needs a leader, especially if you are embarking on a comprehensive entrepreneurial planning and marketing process. Don't expect one of your staff members to take on this task in addition to his or her regular job: A team leader for a typical planning process may have to devote as much as half of his or her time for a year or more. Without that type of focus, the process will drift.

◆ **Create a comfort zone.**
   Once you've recruited the team, take some time to make sure that everybody involved is comfortable with the strategic framework, that they know and agree upon the answers to the following five questions:

   — What is our vision? (How do we want the world to change?)

   — What is our mission? (What will we do to bring about that change?)

   — What are the core values that guide us?

   — What forces are driving us to take part in this process?

   — What outcomes do we expect?

Most nonprofits find it worthwhile to spend one or two meetings at the beginning of the planning process clarifying the answers to these questions and are often surprised at what happens. The "mentors" and "wild cards" (and occasionally the insiders) may challenge some of your most dearly held assumptions and your answers may begin to change.

9. Think like a business at all times

Over the years, social entrepreneurs have learned some harsh lessons about the market. Here are six lessons that apply regardless of whether you are concentrating on current programs or starting something new:

© National Center for Nonprofit Boards

◆ **Find a niche.**
The market can be tumultuous and cruel. To succeed, you *must* have a sound business concept, regardless of whether you're enhancing an internal program or contemplating a spin-off business venture. In other words, you need a market *niche* — a product or service that works, somebody who wants it, and somebody who is willing and able to buy it.

In the nonprofit sector, of course, the last part is frequently the toughest, because the "client" and the "customer" are often two different parties. But, as Paul Hawken says in his book, *Growing a Business*, the goal of any entrepreneurial effort is to reduce your idea to its essence — and then continue reducing it until you find a space that is small enough for you to defend but large enough for you to make a profit.

◆ **Be a player or don't play at all.**
This one takes real courage, and it is best expressed in the advice Peter Drucker gave to Jack Welch. It is very difficult for nonprofits to eliminate programs, but the pain can often be mitigated by finding a home for them in another agency that's better positioned to provide the service — and simultaneously freeing yourself to concentrate on the programs where *you* are better positioned. (See the section titled "Getting Started" on page 16 for an outline of a process that can help you decide which programs to keep and which to shed).

◆ **Price your products and services aggressively.**
Putting an appropriate price on what we do is another aspect of marketing that is equally difficult for people in the nonprofit sector to accept. Nonprofits have been trained over the years to rejoice if they cover costs, much less show a modest profit. But neither of these approaches can help to fund the future or even current overhead.

When setting pricing strategies, nonprofit managers need to think in terms of annual budgets, not just the costs associated with a specific project. For example, successful service companies in this country have a gross profit margin of 40 to 60 percent on everything they sell. They need that *gross* margin in order to finish the year with an overall *net* margin (what remains after overhead, payroll, and other internal and external sales costs are deducted) of three to five percent (the definition of a successful service business). In other words, if it costs one dollar to deliver a service, charge $1.40 to $1.60. Nonprofits need to adopt this same strategy.

Some people call this approach "value pricing". Of course, introducing the concept abruptly would come as a shock to most current payers. Nevertheless, any nonprofit hoping to become increasingly self-sufficient financially will have to consider this approach and, at the very least, begin raising its prices incrementally.

◆ **Stick to your knitting.**
During the late 1970s and early 1980s, a number of nonprofits across the country began to pursue unrelated business income in an attempt to offset the

escalating cuts in federal and state funding. Most of the efforts failed because the nonprofits not only tried to start a business (which was foreign to most of them), but they were also trying to do it in an arena they knew nothing about.

Most of today's social entrepreneurs have therefore abandoned the unrelated business strategy and are concentrating instead on searching for earned income in their core programs. In other words, *there is a direct relationship between mission and money.* And there's an additional benefit as well: Many of the nonprofits that started unrelated businesses in the past were required to pay taxes, but the Unrelated Business Income Tax (UBIT) does not apply to business ventures tied directly to an organization's mission. (See box below).

If nonprofits actually reach the stage of starting a social purpose business venture, it often takes one of two forms:

— **a direct service business** that provides products or services *to* the organization's target population (for example, home care for the elderly), or

— **an affirmative business** that is created specifically to provide four things *for* the organization's target population: real jobs, competitive wages, career tracks, and ownership opportunities.

◆ **Build the right team.**
If you do decide to start a spin-off business venture, it's essential that the leader of your team be a genuine entrepreneur. Over the years, however, it has become apparent to us that *there is a great difference between innovators, entrepreneurs, and professional managers.* Each of these is needed in the evolution of a program or an organization, but at different times, and rarely does an

Unrelated Business Income Tax

Before your nonprofit decides to enter into an entrepreneurial venture, first consider how this endeavor relates to your mission and how it may affect your nonprofit status. A nonprofit tax-exempt organization registered with the Internal Revenue Service (IRS) as a 501(c)(3) must pay Unrelated Business Income Tax (UBIT) if the money-making activity is substantially unrelated to the organization's tax-exempt purposes. For example, an organization with a publishing function writes and sells books on topics related to its mission. It also sells coffee mugs and calendars, but those products may be considered unrelated to its mission and thus may be subject to tax.

A tax-exempt organization can engage in a substantial amount of unrelated business activities so long as the UBIT is accounted for. However, if an organization's profit-making activities consume too much of its resources, or if annual income from unrelated business activities exceeds 20 or 25 percent of total revenue, the IRS may declare that the organization has deserted its tax-exempt purposes and revoke its exemption.

© National Center for Nonprofit Boards

individual possess more than one of the three skills. Innovators develop and field-test prototypes. Entrepreneurs turn prototypes into businesses. And professional managers secure the future.

But even if you find the right person to lead your venture, he or she cannot do it alone. Four out of five small businesses in this country fail during the first three to five years. But six out of seven small businesses started by graduates of the Harvard Business School succeed. Why? Not because they are any smarter, but because they know how little they really know! The first thing Harvard grads do is surround themselves with people who have expertise in their areas of weakness.

The Massachusetts Institute of Technology (MIT) did a study a few years ago tracking 814,000 small businesses through the first eight years of their existence. They found that the survival rate of companies that had at least four people in the brain trust at the beginning was substantially higher than those that had three or fewer. One of the four must be a proven entrepreneur, but too many entrepreneurs try to do everything themselves. It rarely works.

◆ **Be patient.**
Business ventures take time to mature. Here are two more findings from the MIT study:

— Very little growth occurs during the first six years, and

— The product or service provided by the business changes completely at least once during the first eight years.

10. The separation strategy

Entrepreneurial business ventures have to move quickly, and they cannot do so if they are encumbered by bureaucracy. For that reason, any business started by a nonprofit should be kept as separate as possible from the parent organization. In Paul Firstenberg's book *Managing for Profit in the Nonprofit World*, he writes:

> The basic point . . . is that the creation of a successful profit-making component within a not-for-profit environment — the building of a culture-within-a-culture, so to speak — is a difficult business . . . The chances of successfully doing so will be enhanced if the (profit-making) component is, from the outset, clearly labeled as such, and its different objectives and need for a different operating style are recognized from the start . . . The greater the separation in terms of form, staffing, oversight, and location, the greater are the chances that the profit-making component will be able to function with the necessary clarity of purpose and operating style appropriate to its objectives.

Part of a workable separation strategy is a willingness to create an independent board of directors. The board should have no more than six or seven members, and most of them should be outsiders:

◆ Three or four should be proven entrepreneurs,

◆ One should be a person who is in the business of starting businesses (a seed capitalist or an attorney specializing in start-ups),

◆ One should be the senior executive of the parent nonprofit (to serve as the conscience of the new company, but not to become involved in operations), and

◆ One should be a champion from the parent board who is specifically charged with protecting the new venture from interference by either the parent board or staff.

11. *Do* something

You will *never* have all the resources you need. It takes a genuine entrepreneur to act despite the absence of certainty. "Wanna-be" entrepreneurs want to wait until they have the "perfect" plan. But a "pretty good" plan executed with passion today will always defeat a "perfect" plan tomorrow (primarily because there is no such thing as a "perfect" plan!). Don't be afraid to make mistakes. They help to work out the bugs.

12. Be flexible

Finally, a caveat. The last raw material is the ability to improvise. *There is no right way to proceed,* and the laurels will go to the individuals and the organizations that learn how to adapt, quickly. Vice President Hubert H. Humphrey once said something in another context that perfectly describes an entrepreneur: "Things turn out best," he said, "for those who make the best of the way things turn out."

Getting Started

Most nonprofits adopting entrepreneurial strategies prefer to proceed cautiously. Rather than immediately brainstorming new programs or business ventures, they begin by thoroughly sifting through their current programs in search of earned income possibilities and candidates for either expansion or elimination.

One of the tools that has helped them through the process is "The Mission/Money Matrix®" (see box on page 18), designed to help answer two key questions for each program, product, or service.

The "Mission" Question:

What is the *community need* for this product or service?

◆ Is there a **critical** need?

◆ Is there a **substantial** need?

◆ Is it **needed**?

◆ Is there **some** need?

◆ Is there **very little or no** need?

The first step in sorting through your current programs is to assign a "mission" score to each of them — a task that is far tougher than you might imagine. It's relatively easy to count the number of people who need a particular product or service, but how do you decide whether one of them is more critical than another?

© National Center for Nonprofit Boards

Most nonprofits are reluctant to classify anything as less than critical. That isn't surprising: People in the nonprofit sector are driven by a missionary instinct and loathe the idea of turning anybody away. When they see somebody in pain, they try to help. Before too long, however, the organization is stretched far beyond its capabilities.

For that reason, it's important to practice triage when assigning mission scores. Rank programs according to this hierarchy:

5   A *critical* need;

4   A *substantial* need;

3   *Needed*;

2   *Some* need; or

1   *Very little or no* need.

As a rule of thumb, no more than 20 percent of your programs should fall into the "critical" category, no more than 20 percent into the "substantial" category, and so on. Most organizations that follow this approach find the process is simultaneously painful and liberating, because it gives them the permission to be candid. And it's important to carry out the assigned scores to a single decimal point. Notice that there is a great deal of difference between a score of "2.6" and a score of "3.4": they both round off to a score of "3," but each may require additional considerations in the final analysis.

The "Money" Question:

Once you have separated your programs into the five "mission" categories, you are ready to begin the much more complicated process of assigning "money" scores. The key question is this: What is the *earned income potential* for this product or service? And the answer should again be given in terms of a five-point scale.

5   Could we *make a lot* of money?

4   Could we *make some* money?

3   Could we *cover our costs*?

2   Could we *lose some* money?

1   Could we *lose a lot* of money?

In order to assign the correct "money" score, however, you must first gather at least six types of information about each program, product or service:

◆ **What are the critical success factors associated with generating earned income?** The factors will be different for each product or service. The most important elements might be price, convenience, quality, volume, direct mail, access to referral sources, or numerous other possibilities. (For example, one of the most critical factors for an organization providing nonmedical services for the elderly in their homes is the ability to recruit and retain home care aides).

◆ **What environmental forces will have an impact on your ability to generate earned income?**

The Mission/Money Matrix®

		COMMUNITY NEED			
		CRITICAL NEED	SUBSTANTIAL NEED	NEEDED	SOME NEED	VERY LITTLE OR NO NEED
		5	4	3	2	1
EARNED INCOME POTENTIAL	COULD RESULT IN A SUBSTANTIAL PROFIT — 5	DO	DO	DO	DECIDE	DON'T
	COULD RESULT IN SOME LEVEL OF EXCESS REVENUE — 4	DO	DO	DECIDE	DON'T	DON'T
	EARNED INCOME WILL PROBABLY COVER COSTS — 3	DO	DO	DECIDE	DON'T	DON'T
	COULD RESULT IN SOME LEVEL OF DEFICIT — 2	DECIDE	DECIDE	DECIDE	DON'T	DON'T
	COULD RESULT IN A SUBSTANTIAL DEFICIT — 1	DECIDE	DECIDE	DON'T	DON'T	DON'T

© National Center for Nonprofit Boards

The forces could be positive or negative, and they could emerge from any number of sources (demographic, sociological, technological, political). An obvious example during the past few years has been the impact of managed care on health and human service organizations.

◆ **Who are your primary competitors? And how do you rank against them in terms of the critical success factors and environmental forces?**
Many nonprofits have a difficult time identifying their competition, which could come from the for-profit sector, the nonprofit sector, the public sector, or even individuals.

◆ **What is the size and direction of the market?**
How many earned income dollars will be available to pay for your product or service and from what source(s)? Markets have life cycles, and it's important to know in which direction your market is heading.

◆ **What is the potential profitability of your program?**
Nonprofits are often paralyzed when they attempt to determine profitability because they are unable to discover the "true" cost of a program, frequently because they are unsure how to account for the full impact of indirect costs.

◆ **What level of market share can you capture?**
If the size of the market for a particular product or service today is $10 million and you are currently generating $200,000 of revenue from that product or service, then you control two percent of the market: Based on the answers to the first five "money" questions above, can you raise that to five percent in a three-year period? To 10 percent?

Interpreting Your Scores

Once all of the "mission" and "money" questions have been answered, each of your programs can be placed on the matrix and will fall into a cell with one of three labels: Is it a "do," a "don't," or a "decide" program? And what are you going to do about it? Many nonprofits eliminate as many as a third of their programs after completing this process.

◆ **"Do"** — These programs deserve more resources. They score high on both the mission and money scales.

◆ **"Don't"** — These programs should be eliminated. They are either no longer needed or they will cause severe financial damage to the rest of the organization.

◆ **"Decide"** — These programs are those in which the mix of mission and money is inconclusive, and the organization should explore whatever options are necessary to convert them into "do" or "don't" programs (including changes in marketing strategy, collaborations, acquisitions, divestitures, and so on).

A Final Word

Woody Allen penned something a few years ago that sometimes seems to mirror the Hobson's choice confronting people in the nonprofit sector: "More than any other time in history," he wrote, "human beings face a crossroads. One path leads to despair and utter hopelessness . . . the other, to total extinction. Let us pray we have the wisdom to choose correctly."

This booklet has been an attempt to brighten the horizon; to encourage all of us to stop thinking small; to abandon the bastard child syndrome — the feeling that "we don't belong"; to stop underestimating our staff members, our clients, and ourselves. In short, to stop dreaming limited dreams.

But it's important to close with one final warning: Don't start the entrepreneurial process unless the board is in full agreement to move ahead. Many nonprofits are ill-prepared to begin adopting entrepreneurial strategies. Board members and senior executives are increasingly aware that something has to change, but many of them lack the courage, the savvy, and the staying power required to do so.

Before you begin, therefore, it is important to ask yourselves these questions:

◆ Is this something we *really* want to do?

◆ Do we understand the risks and are we willing to take them?

◆ Are we being realistic about possible results?

◆ Is the timing right?

◆ Do we have the right people and are we willing to give them the freedom, responsibility, and authority necessary for entrepreneurial success?

◆ Do we have enough staying power (dollars, time, psychic energy)?

◆ Are we willing to make mistakes?

◆ Are we willing to actually eliminate programs?

Positive answers to these questions will not guarantee success, but they may give you the confidence to proceed. Do your homework, be willing to take some risks, and remember the three-word mantra pioneers such as John DuRand use to encourage newcomers to the field. It is a phrase that captures the underlying philosophy of social entrepreneurs, and you may want to try it yourself. "Profit . . . is . . . good!"

© National Center for Nonprofit Boards

Recommended Resources

Brinckerhoff, Peter C. *Mission-Based Management: Leading Your Not-for-Profit Into the 21st Century.* Dillon, CO: Alpine Guild, 1994.

Brown, Peter C. *The Complete Guide to Money Making Ventures for Nonprofit Organizations.* Washington, DC: Taft Publishing Group, 1986.

Bygrave, William D. *The Portable MBA in Entrepreneurship.* New York: John Wiley & Sons, Inc., 1994.

Collins, James C., and Jerry I. Porra. *Built to Last: Successful Habits of Visionary Companies.* New York: HarperCollins Publishers, Inc., 1994.

DuRand, John. *The Affirmative Enterprise.* St. Paul, MN: MDI Press, 1990.

Emerson, Jed, and Fay Twersky. *New Social Entrepreneurs: The Success, Challenge and Lessons of Non-profit Enterprise Creation.* San Francisco: The Roberts Foundation, Homeless Economic Development Fund, 1996.

Firstenberg, Paul B. *Managing for Profit in the Nonprofit World.* New York: The Foundation Center, 1986.

Hawken, Paul. *Growing a Business.* New York: Simon & Schuster, 1987.

Inc., The Magazine for Growing Companies: P.O. Box 54129, Boulder, CO 80322-4129 (1-800-234-0999).

Shore, Bill. *Revolution of the Heart: A New Strategy for Creating Wealth and Meaningful Change.* New York: Riverhead Books, a division of G.P. Putman's Sons, 1995.

Skloot, Edward (editor). *The Nonprofit Entrepreneur: Creating Ventures to Earn Income.* New York: The Foundation Center, 1988.

Steckel, Dr. Richard, with Robin Simons and Peter Lengsfelder. *Filthy Rich & Other Nonprofit Fantasies: Changing the Way Nonprofits Do Business in the 90s.* Berkeley, CA: Ten Speed Press, 1989.

Trout, Jack, and Al Reis. *The 22 Immutable Laws of Marketing.* New York: HarperCollins Publishers, Inc., 1993.

About the Author

Jerr Boschee has been with The National Center for Social Entrepreneurs since its founding in 1985 and has been its President and Chief Executive Officer since 1990. Mr. Boschee has more than 35 years of experience in the public, private, and non-profit sectors. He is a former executive for Control Data Corporation, has been an executive for both regional and national nonprofits (including the National Center for Voluntary Action), has been managing editor for a chain of newspapers, served as a Peace Corps Volunteer in India, and has been an adjunct professor in the graduate school at the University of St. Thomas. He is a frequent writer, speaker, and trainer in the social service and public policy arenas, is co-founder of The Affirmative Business Alliance of North America, has served as an advisor to nonprofits in Japan and the former Soviet Union, and is the author of a forthcoming book about some of the country's most successful social entrepreneurs. The material contained in this booklet is adapted from a series of speeches by Mr. Boschee about social entrepreneurship and has been revised specifically for board members.

The National Center for Social Entrepreneurs is a nonprofit organization founded in 1985. Its mission is to encourage entrepreneurship throughout the non-profit sector and to help individual nonprofits create or expand social purpose business ventures. More than a thousand nonprofits participate in the Center's introductory seminars each year and more than a hundred receive a variety of on-site consulting services. For more information, contact the National Center for Social Entrepreneurs at 5801 Duluth Street, Suite 310, Minneapolis, MN 55422. Telephone 612-595-0890; fax 612-595-0232; e-mail ncse@socialentrepreneurs.org; website http://www.socialentrepreneurs.org.

© National Center for Nonprofit Boards

658.048
B 7425

99024

LINCOLN CHRISTIAN COLLEGE AND SEMINARY

3 4711 00152 5460